Life Lessons Poems

by

Elece K. McKnight

Copyright © 2014 by **Elece K. McKnight**.
All rights reserved.

No part of this book may be reproduced, stored in a retrieval system, or transmitted by any means, electronic, mechanical, photocopying, recording, or otherwise, without written permission from the author.

Life Lessons Poems

ISBN: **978-0-9913965-1-1**

Book Design and layout
By
Ray's Computer 2000 - rev. 02/10/2014

ACKNOWLEDGEMENTS

Special Thanks to the Creator, the origin of everything including me.

Many thanks to the following that made this work possible:

My parents

My grandfather, the late Allen McKnight,
For the encouragement he gave me.

My loving husband,
Who supported me both internally and externally, financially and with encouragement.

My children,
Who kept reminding me to complete this book.

I would also like to acknowledge those who helped with the creation of this book.

My Husband **Robin McKnight,**
For encouraging me.

My children **Justice, Victorian, Cherish** and **Su-Hyun,**
Who kept reminding me to complete this book and also helped with typing of the book.

Bonnie Raimondi and **Roshan D'Souza Wolff,**
For their kindly suggestions and help.

Ray R. from **Ray's Computer 2000,**
For Word editing and book cover design and layout.

Praise Elece McKnight

I have known Elece McKnight for two years in the Unification Theological Seminary New York City, but couldn't have ever known her deep and loving heart of mother to her family and community, if I had not read her 2nd Poem.

In sum, I would conclude that Sister Elece's Poems depicts her as a person of great trust and I will not hesitate to recommend her creative writings for the upbringing of the younger generation. She certainly possess great wisdom that she acquired in her path of suffering and gaining victory at the end as we can see with fruits in her four girls she is raising in her family.

I would not hesitate to say that: Sister Elece is an experienced hands-on-coach in life that every family would rely on!

Dr. Georges Tegha

This is what I felt I could say about Elece.

Elece McKnight expresses spiritual sensitivity and deep feeling toward her creator, her family and her country,

Zimbabwe in blank verse with the gift of writing that can move the reader to tears.

Roshan D'Souza Wolff

Elece's poems are a breath of fresh air, helping us to appreciate the simple truths of our lives, which are conducted alongside our loved ones amidst the glory of Creation.

Our daily lives are all too hurried, unthinking and unreflecting; her poetry makes us pause and ponder. From evocative poems of nature with the power to transport the reader to a world of vivid color and sensation to reflections on the important themes of our lives - growing up, marriage and children - our emotion and thought are enriched. Elece's life has been a difficult journey and her home country still groans under the weight of suffering, bravely captured in two poems written during her visits to Zimbabwe. Her poems are also a wellspring of expectation for a brighter future fulfilling our longing for a world of peace in these troubled times.

Lance Gardiner, PhD, MA Oxon

The word under pressure to encapsulate truth and beauty powerfully.

These poems by Elece McKnight take our heart on a journey to the unspoken side of sensitivity and given an opportunity to affirm the Benevolence of the created world, despite all the heartaches.

Thank you for adding stepping stones on the never ending journey our Life that gives added texture and color to our experiences.

Marian North

CATHOLIC HERALD
Newspaper on Aug. 21, 2003
Page No. 28 with the following title:
AFTER TROUBLED START IN LIFE, MOTHER FINDS SOLACE IN POETRY

Elece Kunungura McKnight's favorite quote is "God did not give you anything that you can't handle". It's a real testament of faith, coming from the Zimbabwean whose beginnings were as troubled as her native country's.

McKnight, an our Lady of sorrows Elementary school parent, is the fourth of six children. She suffered early the death of her brother and younger sister. Her mother died when McKnight was 6, and her father split up the remaining children, sending them to live with various relatives until he was able to marry when McKnight was 10. Youthful dreams of becoming a missionary faded, and by the time she was 19, she was contemplating suicide. That was a half time ago. Now 38, she's been happily married since 1989 and is the mother of five daughters. And three years ago she finally gave into a life time of wishing and made a dream come true instead: she started writing poetry.

*"I've been interested in writing since high school, but did not have the chance for many years", she said.
Her first book, self–publishing volume titled "into the millennium", (sic) appeared in 2002.*

With five children ages 10 and under, one might wonder when she found the time to write.

*"Actually, almost all of them I would write at 2 or 3 in the morning", McKnight said, laughing." When I would wake up to feed the baby, put the baby down, I would write something, that's how I did it".
Many of the poems have religious themes. McKnight said she didn't plan it that way.*

When I was writing, I didn't think it was very, very religious," But because it was from inspiration, when I started reading it, I found things that were very religious. Sometimes I look out at the window and think about how beautiful the stars are or the moon is, and just starts flowing. I don't know if I was going to sit down and think about that I could do that.

BY CANDY CZERNICKI
CATHOLIC HERALD STAFF

Contents

Part I	15
001-If I Can Live 1000 Years	16
002-Israel the Beautiful	17
003-Insane Woman	18
004- Naming My Children	19
005-When Our Rabbit Died	20
006-When My Credit Card Took Control	21
007-It Was Sad Enough	22
008-It Was So Lonely	23
009-When They Were Here	24
010- Why You Didn't Wait	25
011-Dialogue…Child To Child	26
012- I Have Company	27
013-At Home Mom	28
014-My Secret Parent	30
015-I'm Glad to Be Me	31
016-From Afar	32
017-Instead Of Getting Bored	33
018-Painful Truth	34
019-Only Time I Went Pale	36
020-When I Ask	37
021-My Pubic	38
022-I'm a Princess	39
023-My Cup of Tea	40
024-Why I Write	41
025-Asking Why	42
026-A Writers Heart	43
027-Pen on Paper	44
028- I Have a Dream	45
029- While I'm living?	46
030-Beyond Time and Space	47
031-Original Colors Together	48
Part II	50
001-Gelatin Love	52
002-My Husband	53

003-My Sacred Present	54
004-I Cry For My Country	55
005-Resume for My Daughter	58
006-The Map of My Life	59
007-I Was Only A Child	60
008-When Home Was No Longer Home	62
009-It Was Always Someone	63
010-Freedom River	64
011-Christmas 1976	66
012-Upraise In the City	68
013-One Day Enough Was Enough	69
014-Panic Attack	70
015-I Wanted To Close My Eyes	71
016-Now I Can See	72
017-The Battle Fields	73
018-As I Faced My Brother	74
019- Ignorance, Yes It Makes Sense	76
020-Aren't You My Brother/ Sister?	77
021-Still in Control	78
022-Battling To Fit In	79
023-I Know You Love Me So Much	80
024-Can't You See and Hear Africa	82
025-Who Was Calling This Time	84
026-Where I Receive Love	85
027-When I Went Somewhere	87
028-As I Was Graduating	88
029-Aren't You Ashamed	90
030-Trip to the Kingdom Of Hell	91
Part III	94
001- This Is Not My Home	95
002-Somewhere I Call Home	96
003- Truth	97
004-Its Only Here on Earth	98
005- Not Up To Me	99
006-Not Because	100
007-Agony of the Unknown	101
008-Why Is It So Difficult To Understand	102
009-I Starved You	103
010-Aren't You My Brother/Sister?	104

011-Supposing To Be	105
012-Essence of Life	106
013-The Original Mind	107
014-The First Great Authors	108
015-Freedom of My Mind	109
016-Priority	110
017-Body Specialist	111
018- Waiting for Jesus	113
019- In Place Of	114
020- When I Opened My Eyes	115
021- Forever Reunion	116
022- Once Upon a Time	117
023-A Trip to the Kingdom Of Heaven	118
024-Getting High with the Most High	119
025-The River	120
026-Thank You God	121
027-In His Bowl	122
028-I Thought This Is It	123
029-God Given Credentials	124
030-A World of Thought	125
031-Is He There	126
032-What a Miserable God I'm	127
033-When I Turned Of All Lights	128
034-I'm Blind	129
035-Why Black And White	130
036-Old Self	132
037-Rather Take a Path	133
039- This Little Light of Mine	136
040-Gathered For the Word	137
041-Slave to a Belief	139
042-The Source	140
043-The Original Mind	141

Part I

Religious and Spiritual

From the Author:

Beyond all the barriers that we might have, in nationality, race and creed, we still hold some spiritual values.

We all, at one point or another, walk the same path.

001-If I Can Live 1000 Years

Being meant to live until ready to leave
Was the order of creation?
Going whining, regretting feeling
Sorry not the order of creation
If I can, not from God

Creation and the world for me
Ready to be seen and experienced
If I could only live 1000 years or more

180 countries and cultures to be seen
Countless complexities to wander about
Languages to learn
Lessons of every kind to learn
Responsibilities to carry
Just let me live 1000 years or more
Accomplishments to be made
With limitless abilities
With more years to learn
I only wish I could live 1000 years.

*****

002-Israel the Beautiful

Hills and valleys around
Overlooking Jerusalem
City of history
History that can't be comprehended
History of every kind
From the mosaic to the wars of today
Trails of historical footsteps
Here the good and evil is expressed
Expressed in every kind
Masculine and feminine expressed together

The hills are the masculinity of the creator
Whereas valleys are lush and green
A welcoming environment for all
Where everyone wants to live
Leaving the deserted area
Thus the femininity of God

*****

003-Insane Woman

Always on the same corner
Cleaned and well dressed

My first impression was,
She is waiting for the bus
Since she dances to the music
All the time, I just thought she loves music

After observing numerous times
I realized, thus insane

I began to notice more things
Sometimes she made motions
Like she is waving at someone then she seems
Like an argument is going on,
Then like she is running after the person
Then she stops holds her fists like she is preparing for a fight
All this was in segments of just minutes

She is in both worlds physical and spiritual.
Thus the insane woman

*****

004- Naming My Children

No wonder there is craziness around
Every child seems to be possessed by the unknown spirit
Now they have to find out a name
For the unnatural behaviors
They call it ADD
Now they are in business
Selling ADD medicine
Still naming my children

My children are children not kids
Can you imagine a child being a kid!!!
A kid!? a goat
As wild as they are
Who can take care of kid?
I took care of sheep, cows, donkeys but not goats
They flip flops and kicks
There are kids
But not my children
They are children
No more naming and children

*****

005-When Our Rabbit Died

I remember my husband saying
That rabbit had died.
I looked at him with great surprise I asked why?
He said, he doesn't know.
I didn't think again until we got home
Surely the rabbit was dead

Just the ten days we were away,
Our rabbit died.

It was a family member now
It ate what we ate
As I peel and cut vegetable, I think about it
I feel lost without our rabbit
I miss our rabbit so much that I still call Harper,
This was its name
I truly miss our rabbit

*****

006-When My Credit Card Took Control

Thought I'm in control
Getting what I need when I need it
They even showed how important I was
By giving me more cards
Gratefully I accepted every one of them

I started wanting to do what the Johns do.
Glamour, clothes, matching head to toe
Taking exclusive vacations
Christmas time was the best
I just simply maximize every one of those cards

Time for the bills, I started paying one credit card with the other
Like they say borrowing from Peter to pay Paul
Still thinking I'm handling it.

Finally I couldn't remember what I was paying for.
I worked to pay credit cards.
God said "Have dominion over all things"
And yet all things were having dominion over me
What a reversal of dominion.

*****

007-It Was Sad Enough

I did not believe it
I tried to stay away from it
I did not want it to be a part of me
So I ignored it

Internally little by little I believed it
How queer believing something I didn't want to believe

It was like a cancer
Destroying me silently
And yet I was still in denial
In truth it was mere ignorance
Because the spirit had already excepted it

One day I came out of that shell
Real! a big blanket
The blanket that covered me for my entire life

I heard from a distance,
You are a girl you really can't do that
Some jobs are for men
Girl's jobs are to be married
Take care of the family
Girls shouldn't really go to school
For what?
Its wasting money
I heard every voice, mockery
Teasing, denouncing and even angry
I knew then I was trapped
When I heard it enough
Enough was enough
*****

008-It Was So Lonely

I remembered when I was five.
When November came, we prepared to go
It was grandma's house
Many families would gather
It was merry.
Turkey, dressing, pies every kind and cookies
Most of all was the joy of being together

This time, I heard Radio, TV announcing
Thanksgiving
I knew what thanksgiving is like,
But I knew also
I wouldn't have it that way

It was a different year
Things have changed
Family grew apart
Pain and frustration filled my heart
I knew then how lonely
It's going to be.

*****

009-When They Were Here

My eyes were weary,
Day after day I looked the same
It was from cooking, cleaning, washing, diapers and
school activities
Also the recreational classes

I was always in the state of giving up,
But I couldn't
I wished I could share the responsibility
but their was no one to share with
Time to sleep was the most cherished
I come to realize how precious sleep is

Sometimes grandma would call,
Her famous question was; what is everyone doing?
Honestly the answer was, I don't know.
Since I couldn't say that, I had to narrate one by one.

Then I started, Justice is watching TV,
Victorian is in the bathroom, Cherish is sleeping and
Su-hyun is playing with a doll.
This was a typical day in the house
When they were at home

*****

010- Why You Didn't Wait

Why you didn't wait
To see me going through all the stages in life
At least until adulthood
Passing through the teen stages
With all its challenges
Why you didn't wait?

I went on for years not so sure
If you were gone
When times were hard,
I always thought, I would feel a back rub
Letting me know, things will be all right
With the love you wished to express, so
Why you didn't wait

I prepared surprises for you
To share and enjoy
The joy of your grandchildren
My accomplishments in life
I wished you could have waited to see
What life heard for you from me?
I truly can't figure that out
Why you couldn't wait

*****

Life Lessons Poems   *Elece McKnight*

011-Dialogue...Child To Child

6 yr. Old: I wonder why on all the videos the people never change their clothes.

5 yr. Old: Ah! I bet you those clothes must smell.

6 yr. Old: Yes. For a hundred years I have watched them and you know what, they also talk the same things, walk the same way every time, and they're in the same place

4 yr. Old: I think it's so boring.

8 yr. Old: You silly dummy, don't you know that's just a video?

6yr, 5yr, 4 yr. So-o-o-o-o

8 yr. Old: The video was taped the same time the people were wearing those clothes. The video is just a picture.

5 yr. Old: Picture! How come they are moving? Our pictures on the wall never move or talk.

6 yr. Old: And you know what? Some of those people grow.

8 yr. Old: Well. You don't understand, just ask mum then.

A true Conversation of my children

*****

012- I Have Company

7:00 a.m. hello?
Who is there
Oh! How are you?
Aha yea, yes. Ok bye.
8:00 AM. Hello! Oh Joan
Where are you
Ok, O, yes, fine
Bye
12:00 PM. hello! Liz, are you ok?
I have been on the phone with Roger
And Joan
I'm just fine how about you?
Alright
Thanks.
1:00 PM hello, May I know who is calling?
No thank you.
Ok
Good bye.
3:00 PM hello! May I know who is calling?
I will send $10.00 this month
Bye.
5:00 PM hello! Oh Robin
You will be home soon
Thus my companion
All day I spent on it
What about life.
*****

013-At Home Mom

Not only did my husband wander,
But me too
What did I do too?
What did I do today?
What did I do all day?

I remember being tired every day,
My back aching, but still,
I couldn't recall why?

9 o'clock a.m., everyone is gone,
Toys shoes, towels, combs and clothes,
Were from the entrance door to the bedrooms
Then I started picking up everything
Moping, sweeping, scrubbing, etc
Before I realize, it was 12 noon,
My youngest need to be picked up from school
Come back another snack and then more mess to be cleaned

And of course everyone has a story to tell
I didn't eat my lunch it was yak,
I didn't have free time,
Someone was teasing me.
I have to sit and listen

Then time for homework.
In between finish dinner

Dinner is ready at 6p.m.
Following is bath time
Then prayer and bed time

It's quiet; I look at the house,
I ask, what did I do all day
From the entrance to the bedrooms,
Shoes, pencils, sweaters, clothes towels
Just the way it was at 8a.m.

I started all over again,
Picking sweeping, mopping and so on
10 p.m., I'm sitting in bed
What did I do all day?

*****

014-My Secret Parent

I felt loved and being comforted
Without fail I listened and attended them
It was like I had everything
Only stood up for bathroom breaks and eating
Though 'am learning all I needed to learn

It was a seven days a week /24hrs a day
There was so much variety, that I hated missing anything
It was just as religious as it could be
If I didn't attend, I felt guilt

They felt doing me a favor
Inside I was being destroyed
And robbed of my creativity
And the dignity I deserve
THE MEDIA AND THEIR TV'S

*****

015-I'm Glad to Be Me

I can't help but feel glad
They joy, happiness thus for me
Though sometimes challenging
But when I think deeply, I'm glad to be me

The unique individual me
With no one in the world like me,
I'm so thankful and grateful to be me

I know there is controversy
Some think I'm nothing
While others work 24/7 to disapprove anything to do with me
But I'm glad to be there as I'm
To be the whole unique individual being

My brothers and sister
So unique too
Their ways and deeds so different from mine
Are they right or wrong?
And thus why I'm glad just to be me
I offer what I'm supposed to
Do the best I know how to
Serve to the best I know, how too
Willingly and unconditionally
Thus why I say I'm glad to be me
*****

016-From Afar

Looking from a distance
Nothing is the same
The shape, size and appearance all different
When looking from a distance

The skies seem to have the ending
The stars
The moon
The sun
And all planets,
They look extremely small
Yet very huge
Thus when you look from afar

The sun only gives enough heat
The moon just enough light
And thus only from a distance
Coming closer things are different

*****

017-Instead Of Getting Bored

I took the chance
To reflect and meditate
Placing my mind where it belongs
Connecting with my inner self
Regaining the lost treasures of life
Instead of getting bored

Dreaming about the future
Planning my goals
And moving along with them
Not sitting and eating
In fact I never really get bored but frustrated
For there is not enough time in a day

Instead of getting bored,
I see myself pacing trying to beat the rush hr. of time
I did and accomplish more
Instead of getting bored.

*****

018-Painful Truth

I can just imagine mom and dad
In that ward, when the nurse announced,
Oh thus a handsome baby boy
I could just see them glance at each other's,
And smile with joy

Taking myself back when I was 5, 10,15,
All the way to 17
Going into the boys clothing stores
Closets filled with boys toys games etc.

Though strange feelings pressing on me,
I stayed non-guilty me.

At 18 the doors were opened.
DO WHATEVER YOU WANT
BE WHATEVER YOU WANT
ACT ANYWAY YOU WANT

Well!!! With all the help I need,
Now I'm in a dress, long pressed hair,
Nail polish on and lipstick on.
Make matters worse, now I'm Lizzie instead of Larry
Families are confused and worried.
I even accepted to be called a wife.

Life Lessons Poems   *Elece McKnight*

Sometimes I sit, take my inner self all the way back,
I cry like a baby
I have to live with this PAINFUL TRUTH

*****

019-Only Time I Went Pale

Nothing would get me that far
To be in some illusion state
Imagining something out of my control
Seeing myself other than what I am

These were the imagines
White, yellow, blue, red etc.
All not real
No white, yellow, blue, red
Thus only when I went pale

*****

020-When I Ask

I thought it being the best way
So I ask
Not knowing how different we are,
I ask
Each time I ask,
I get different answers
All I ask was the same question
Expecting one same answer

My wish was clarity
So I ask
More confusion comes
I started wondering
Why? When I ask

Can't there be one universal understanding
It's always like that when I ask
Thus why I ask
But thus what I get each time
Why ask

*****

021-My Pubic

It was just overnight
All was different
I started to notice development
Physically and emotionally
I wasn't sure what this was.
Feeling of wander and lost filled me
Emotionally it was bothersome
I wanted to understand myself more deeply
I started to ask questions

Who am I?
Why am I here
Who created this world?
What is my purpose of being here?

With this I started
A new search into "the origin"

*****

022-I'm a Princess

Eyes upon me
Admiring everything about me
Everyone believes happiness lies within me
Yet, so little they know about me

Wherever I go they watch me
Believing they were protecting me
When I come outside, I have a troop by my side
Surely misery was upon me

Approaching other kids to play
They whisper to each other,
"There she comes."
Silence was in the air
Wondering whether to play with me or not
They also believed I had everything I needed

I often wondered and asked myself a question,
"Is everything all right with me?"
Upon discovering the natural human desire
Of mutual giving and receiving
I realized I'm the princess
Without the peace

A reflection of Princess Diana

*****

023-My Cup of Tea

Not because I need it
Not because it was sweet
Has cream and sugar
Not because it was healthy
As a matter of fact, it has caffeine

All because it makes my transaction period smooth
All because it was soothing
All because I can reflect on my last chore
All because I couldn't drink it like a glass of water

So I had to sit there and sip
And I can taste every ingredient in it
What a great way to start and finish my day

*****

024-Why I Write

It wasn't for only joy
But to share
Sharing importance in life
Not from me
But from Thy Father

He asked me to share
I heard no voice
No authority
And no power
I knew then,
No any other way, but to write

No concerns of status
Not everyone knows me personally
No string of credentials
Except what Thy Father gave to me
I then started to write

No limits
No power needed
No authority to approve
No credential, besides,
I know how to hold a pen and write
I then fulfill the desire to share
I then write
*****

025-Asking Why

Though it sounds strange, or funny,
But it is the way of life.
In all what we have to do,
Asking why we should be normal.

Sometimes you feel out of place,
Or you feel rejected
For asking why

People think you should
Know without asking.
But hey, you don't know, so ask why?

They will come asking to drink, smoke, and have sex,
Just remember life itself has a purpose
So there is nothing thus going to happen without a purpose
So, ask yourself "WHY"

*****

026-A Writers Heart

A lonely path
Impulse to give
Sharing limitless
Hoping for the best results
That every reader can gain something
Thus a non-stop career

Sometimes fear leads the way
Fear of rejection
Sometimes of great success
Not knowing the pros and cons of either one
Thus the writer's heart

*****

027-Pen on Paper

As I put the pen on paper
The whole world opened up
Hidden treasures are revealed
Beginning to see that in and out of this world
Realizing also that I'm the center of it
As I begin to write
Scenes seem to appear
All words begin to come
Words of fear, love, hesitant, hate
All just flow

As the writing goes on
Reflections of happy and sad moment
It's a healing process
It's like going through the similar situation
This time with a different look

*****

028- I Have a Dream

I believe they will come true.
I hope and yearn for the day
For them to come true
I wasn't confident about it before
But now I believe they
Will come true
One thing I needed,
Determination
It is the key to my dreams
There were many I saw coming true.
I saw them unfolding.
Since I was little girl
I've seen many come true.
They really do come true.

*****

029- While I'm living?

It's hard to imagine
To say when or where
Who and how
Being easy as A, B, C
Or 1, 2, 3
What can I do while I'm living?
I have a mouth to talk with
I have hands and feet to
Serve others,
I have eyes to see
And a brain to think
I can use all these for the good
It's impossible to do later.
It is impossible to do later.
And hard to imagine doing
It in the hereafter
Only while I'm living
Realize after,
Regrets after,
Repentance after,
All these are not good as
While I'm living

*****

030-Beyond Time and Space

I knew it wasn't that simple
I knew too it was my responsibility
And also just for me only

Away from myself I departed
Realization of the universe
And its reality
I wept upon
Viewing its sight

It was like a slide show
One picture after the other
I went from country to country

These are the pictures
In one place, hunger was
Sweeping the country,
Floods, sickness, war, abuse
Tears were rolling down from
Different people for different reasons
I saw every color, race, class, and background

Under one umbrella
I realize one thing, One World, One people,
And overall, the same reality

*****

031-Original Colors Together

The flowers, the trees all have colors
Colors of all different kinds
Colors that change
According to time, weather and season

Despite their differences
Can grow side by side
In the same garden or fields
In harmony and peace
Our own botanical gardens,
Filled with flowers of all different colors
Red, pink, purple, black blue yellow orange green
etc…

All in the same garden
That gives joyful and peaceful atmosphere
The original colors are these
White, black, and yellow
This is the original Eden
Where everything shall be in harmony

*****

Life Lessons Poems   *Elece McKnight*

Life Lessons Poems   *Elece McKnight*

Part II

Seeking Happiness And Fighting Battles

From the Author:

> **While we all desire to acquire happiness nevertheless we suffer greatly fighting the internal battles. This battle is the battle of the mind and body.**

Life Lessons Poems   *Elece McKnight*

001-Gelatin Love

Attractive, Colorful and soft
Shaped in a basin bowl
Can be molded in any shape
It is molded in any shape
It is that fragile

If the shape is destroyed
Can't be reshaped
Thus the nature of gelatin

Real love is strong and unchangeable
Can't be sharped
In another form
Can't be changed nor transferred
Its internal is solid like a rock

*****

002-My Husband

Weather rainy and sunny
Thy God's presences in thee
Beneath thy heart lies thy love

Thou shaken, yet thy stand
Times of hunger,
Thy presence was manna from heaven
When thirsty
Thy love was like showers of blessings
During temptation,
Yet thy persevere
Times of doubt,
Thy instill faith

Thy most high spoke through thy husband
Thou shall live eternity together
Thus said thy God

*****

003-My Sacred Present

Placed on the most sacred position
Years and years was securely locked
In a sacred place
With a sacred key
Set aside for a special person
No unauthorized person is to open
Only one key is given
To the authorized person

Faithfully I avoided all temptations
Avoiding the ones who wanted to break in
I choose death than to let go
Opening without the key is a violation
Exposing it is a sin

This precious gift for you
Its beauty so special to be cherished
Not everyone but by only one person
When opening it, joy and beauty
Lies within
All heaven glorify to the beauty

*****

004-I Cry For My Country

Lush lands still stretches across the horizon
Mountainous, rocky and ever green
It was the land that was loved by many
It was the land of opportunity

Streets were clean and fearless
Villages filled with the rich traditions
Loving one another as brothers and sisters

Plagues of every kind
Drought
Floods
Diseases sweep the land
Orphans as old as 10 years or less to take care of themselves
Looking around, or across, I couldn't help, but
CRY, CRY, CRY!!!
Feeling of hopelessness, dismay, desperation and discontentment
Filled my heart
I cried as I looked around
The desire to help was endless
The help I can't describe
Help of every kind
I cried to get the curse taken away
Upon my beloved country, that I loved until now
I found myself asking God, are you there

Life Lessons Poems   *Elece McKnight*

If so please release the curse

Countless times, I was warned,
BE CAREFUL, BE CAREFUL!!!
Of my brothers and sisters
Unreasonably desperation created sinful hearts

Sure to sell urine as perfume or cooking oil
Just to get one meal
Standing on corners plotting robbery
Black marketing of every kind
Officials leading the way
Order is destroyed
Beautiful flats and suburbs are now market places
Littering on every corner
Heavy metal doors with big padlocks as if the house
is a garage
The fear has reached every heart

I cried as I looked around
For the same places I used to know are in vain
I still cry for my country

On the other hand,
The world's quality artists are reviled
Creativity is growing
Arts I never saw before
Now through the natural resources,
Natural beauty still maintains itself

Life Lessons Poems   *Elece McKnight*

Rivers refilled its species
Balancing rocks of its kind
The Victoria falls that never fades

Ranges of mountainous stretches through the land

At times I sit and contain myself
But mostly I CRY, CRY AND CRY
Cry for my beloved country ZIMBABWE

Written during my visit to Zimbabwe May 2003

005-Resume for My Daughter

Not so sure how to handle the pressures of growing
up
I thought and thought and thought
I realized, there should be a way
She looked a dazzling heart-breaking teen
Resume was the solution
Yes resume, I reassured myself

I started a list of all the qualifications
It was a lot of no's
No smoking, drinking beer, fooling around
And a thorough screening of the background
E.g. job, and believes.
Whoever wants to have the blessing of marriage?
I just say resume
It was new, yes but it was new to me too
So I felt safe to say "Resume"

*****

006-The Map of My Life

It's like a quilt
With different patches
Designs and colors
Can be as big and colorful as the designer wishes
As well as beautiful and adorable
Can be used or discarded
Can be attractive as resource
For others to find direction
In this chaotic and confused world

Let the map glow
Brighter and clearer
Let it be used with love and care
Let the world see it

*****

Life Lessons Poems *Elece McKnight*

007-I Was Only A Child

Being left at six
Though normal to others but not for me
Since I was just a child

I guess they thought I should know and understand
Also to act responsibly for myself
But I was only a child six years old

Transformed into a new world
Filled with darkness, despair, and hopelessness
Roaming around with feelings of being rejected

Yes unknowingly I accepted my new life
Since I was only a child
I expected to be fed,
Cleaned, and taught manners,
But all was in vain
Irresponsibly they ignored me
And yet I was only a child

I started getting signals of different things
Reminders of me being an orphan were vivid
I felt lost
Unfairly treated
And unworthiness that still haunts me today
Though I was just a child

Life Lessons Poems *Elece McKnight*

Looking back,
Could I have done better?
Acted better?
Understood better and responded better?

Maybe so, but remember I was just a child.

*****

008-When Home Was No Longer Home

It was the same place in my mind
The area I grew up and know very well
I used to called it home
Home is the distinctive word
The elements and functional statues of a place
Where there was the head of the home
There was stability and dignity
The place was home

When I think dad,
I imagine home
The one I used to call home
It is no longer home
The elements are gone
Thus mom and dad
Thus I visualize as home

A place now filled with sorrow and grief
Orphans running around
In their minds still calling the place home
When actually it's only a dream now
For me it's a place I used to call home

*****

009-It Was Always Someone

No, never me
Not me
But the boss
My husband, my wife
My neighbor
My teacher
My workmate

It so happened that no one was around
Then, it was the dog
My job
My house
The tree at the backyard
The clothes that I have
My car
And of course about anything
It never be me, but someone

*****

010-Freedom River

Long and wide it stretches,
Beauty that can't be appreciated
Watchful eyes from both ends

Feelings of endless hope capture their attention
To be reunited in peace and harmony
Each in loneliness cries
Fatal souls in the same sorrow
Longing for descendants to be together

Who can hear their cries of each other
Who can walk the same path?

Who can understand the deep sorrowful desire of these children?

Who can wish to walk the desert path like Israelites who longed for their deliverance?

In their desperate wish, they hoped for the day,
The day of hope

Who can be the hope, for the long separated children of Korea?

Who can be the deliverer?

Life Lessons Poems *Elece McKnight*

Who can be their hope?

Who can be their Messiah?

It is a reflection when I went to 38th parallel in Korea.
The river divides the South and North Korea

*****

011-Christmas 1976

Deep in the countryside of Chipinge
Just like anywhere else
Adults and children all count days

Whether Christ was honored or not
Most of the excitement was centered on different reasons
The most positive thing was happiness

Naked bodies will be dressed
The yearly dresses, suits, and shoes will be coming
The food will be different too
Thus the day for rice and chicken in abundance
Tea, bread, and butter
Soft drinks as one could take
This sounds like everyday things
No. Not in the countryside of my hometown

All the dreams were shattered Christmas 1976
Zimbabwe was in war
I had seen everything so close about the war
Three days before the big day
The soldiers flooded the land
They were dropped like raindrops
All we heard was noise all over
Before we could think, they were at our door
All they said was pack and go

Life Lessons Poems *Elece McKnight*

We couldn't ask any questions but to obey

We could only take so much
Mainly food and a few clothes

We were driven like heads of cattle's
Men pointing at us,
Each family with two or more soldiers to accompany them
Our area was called the protected villages
It was a fenced area about five blocks long
And our new home was nothing more than a piece of ground
All we could do for shelter was
Putting plastic paper over the roof
Rain was pouring
All the food was wet
Our best food was ruined
We did not have anywhere to cook due to the rain
The internal and external were ruined

December 25, 1976

*****

012-Uprise in the City

It was famous and well known for its integrity
Filled with all the educated and well known noble
man and woman
No one knows how it started
All of a sudden there was confusion

People were rushing to all different directions
Some screaming and shouting
No one could understand what was being said
Bumping and pushing each other
Important papers flying in all directions
No one was trying to ask for help
Since everyone seemed to know what was going on

People rushed in anything that was open
Houses, cars garages and bathrooms
No one was able to recognize their own property
All what mattered was survival
Since no one knows how it started
No one knows how it ended
It just went on and on!!!

*****

013-One Day Enough Was Enough

He holds on for the past 20 years
I didn't dream of it happening
Fights and arguments were a routine
It was like tragic without our routine
It felt like something was surely wrong

One day enough was enough
He packed his belongings and he was gone
For memory he left razors, shaving cream and off course
A forever memory "CHILDREN"

I was lost in space
Still in a great denial
I wandered through the whole house
Turning myself into reality

All the goodness I never knew about him
Starts to unfold
It felt like I was watching a film of my life
The regrets I felt couldn't help
I wished, I wished it could never happen this way
But enough was enough

*****

014-Panic Attack

There is a person there!!
They are going to steal
They are coming closer

Let's protect ourselves
Guns and other weapons are prepared
It's all for that person there
Who is that?
Everyone is doing the same
So who is coming to attack who?

Finally the guns are in the wrong hands
Now the real time to be afraid
Since someone will be coming
For the real attack

*****

015-I Wanted To Close My Eyes

Day after day I hear and saw
Mostly terrifying and pitiful sights

I turned on the TV, three quarter of the news
Accident, shooting, kidnapped, raped, and so on
Looking was a pity

I thought to try the radio
It was equally the same
Terrifying, scary, intimidating, and shameful

Finally I decided to relate to people only
Again I wished I could just go deaf and blind
Sorrow and misery was being expressed
As though the whole story would be told through the skin

Come to listen, I wanted to bury myself alive
Thus when I decided to close my ears and eyes

*****

016-Now I Can See

Things were happening around me
I would just walk away and ignore
Just like nothing is going on
I felt like I was living in my own world
Shattered from the rest of the world

Wars, slavery, bigotry, jealousy
Gossipy, racism, and hatred
I see and hear but I couldn't really see or hear
I felt fighting any endless battle within myself
Two minds battling to make the decision of right or wrong
I was in-between two worlds
Until I could hear and see

Though I thought I saw and heard, but I could not see or hear
One day I realized the truth
I started seeing and hearing the truth
My world was opened to the truth
It was the truth that made me see and hear
And now I see and hear

*****

017-The Battle Fields
I listened and learned
I affirmed myself with hope.
I believed in all I was told
But the battle had started

The TV, radio, newspaper, etc.
All confirmed they were wrong
We have to fight
While the battle was going on I agreed
I prepared to retaliate
Though the battle was going on

They had two legs, two arms, a head, two eyes, and skin
I knew thus my brothers/sister
As I prepare to face my brother/ sister
Ready to slaughter them
Ignoring the battle that was going on

In the battlefield was war
The war that everyone could see
Yet inside me was another war
War between mind and body
And that of good and evil
I did as I was told
Yet the battle goes on

This time was worse
I could hear their cries and they die
The sorrowful groaning
The war became worse and worse
I was dying in my battlefield
Yet still trying to hold
*****

018-As I Faced My Brother

Inside was something
Retreating and repellent
Blood and sweat I shed
Realizing what was ahead

I could have seized then and there
But there was something inside

Pride, arrogance, ignorance, filled my heart
Knowing the consequences I continue
Ignoring my family and kin
Believing this is God's will

I really could have stopped it
Simply admitting my realization
That I was innocent and small
But since I waited so long
I can't go back

Could have been better looking stupid than acting likewise
I cried inwardly

Wanting to admit how small and innocent I was
But my tongue was held
I went ahead and faced my brother
It wasn't the big things

Life Lessons Poems *Elece McKnight*

Little do you realize how I felt?
Just that thought
This was more than a thought
It was a realization

Thanks a lot

*****

019- Ignorance, Yes It Makes Sense

Tried to use the reasons I have
When they chained me, stole from me, even starved me
It only makes sense when I say its ignorance

Human beings have feeling
And feel sympathy, compassion, and love
And yet nothing seems to be present
Thus when I say its ignorance
Then it makes sense

I watched all the wicked around me
Killing like they are slaughtering a cow for pleasure
Abusing all categories
Despising, fooling, cheating, jealousy, etc
And you know what?
They swear they are innocent
Thus when it makes sense to say
Its ignorance

*****

020-Aren't You My Brother/ Sister?

Whole heartedly I believe you are a brother. Sister
When I looked at you
I see a brother and sister
You know what
You have a head, abdomen, legs, toes and fingers
And a face with eye, a nose, a mouth, and ears
And thus what I have too

When you are mistreated and you cry, those clear
tears, I feel the same and you know what? I have the
same tears too
A mom and dad conceived you
Carried in the womb for nine months
Delivered the normal way
And you know what? I was too

I can go on and on, but you know what?
I really believe you are my brother/ sister

*****

021-Still in Control

Hallelujah its freedom
Freedom from slavery
Freedom from segregation
And freedom from everything else
And yet still in control

Control of my life, job, and my talent
Yes where do I go for jobs or to improve my talent?
Thus still in control isn't it?

I know my talents and my ability
For as long as my memory allows me years back
Who are the CEO's of every company?
Still in control

I hopped from one place to another
Looking for that long longed freedom
Freedom to gain the freedom of my life
Yet still in control

As much as I try to ignore
Acting as religious as I could be
My life is kept like stagnant water
Why? Still in control

*****

022-Battling To Fit In

I was so much in denial
Of the reality and the truth that existed
So I did everything it took
Though inside it was a lot
Trying to be a part

At times I felt success
But other times total failure
The desire was so strong
So I kept pushing

It was in every area
Socially, racially, and economically
Some aspect I could change
While others were impossible to change
At times I felt like the many century cursed Ham

I tried to move from place to place
From job to job
Still the battle was the same
I then realized it was an endless battle
Only one kind of person
And that was I
And the battle to fit in was over.

*****

023-I Know You Love Me So Much

It was clear that you admired how charming and admiring I was

That I was gifted to use both sides of my brain
That I had the awesome opportunity and responsibility

To have a special womb
That is blessed to carry children
That my body structure takes
Man's breathe away

Some even pass out as I dash in
Man became so creative
In order to win my heart

That voice was that angelic vocal chord
I know all that, but how
Could you think you can be me?
Then you started imitating me
The walk
The talk
That wasn't so bad, but when
You thought you could change your gender
And the way you dress
Oh and the makeup
I thought thus too far

Life Lessons Poems   *Elece McKnight*

And listen, you even took it further
When you decided to marry
Someone just like you
And agreed to be called a wife
And I know you love me
But not to that extent

*****

024-Can't You See and Hear Africa

Eyes open wide
Seeing but can't see
All that's going on around you
Can't you see?

Our history has no hidden icons
It's just an open book
Tales of our ancestors
Grandpa with as many wives
As he can afford
Well it wasn't free and you know
All lived in the same yard as sisters
Can't you hear and see that history?

Grandpa hopped from one wife to another his entire life
Of course, having sex
And yet lived more than 100 years
Grandpa died of old age
Can't you hear and see?

Today all I hear is Aids
What is that?
Diseases caused by having too many sexual partners
Can't you see and hear?

I can't. I can't. I can't.

Life Lessons Poems   *Elece McKnight*

I can't accept this

Why? Why? Why lord?
Why today?
Today babies are said to have Aids

And a well-crafted statement is put together
In order to justify the deed
Among came cures, but what happened was never told
Can't you hear and see?

Open those eyes
It means death
The land is in dismay
Smell of death across the land

Since they have developed a name for everything
They said it was HIV Aids
Said to be from multiple sexual relationships
But why today?

*****

025-Who Was Calling This Time

The phone call were not the normal ones
I mean the ones that comes from maybe 9am-9pm
It was the ones that comes from 2am-5am
In my deep sleep I woke
Hesitantly reaching to the receiver
A string of questions in my mind
My sister, cousin or nephew or niece
With a timid voice, hello

Again was my sister
With the same news for a different person
This was my uncle
He is very sick.
Few hours later was an email
He is dead

This wasn't the first time
It happened but rather to a different person
Hope is lost.

*****

Life Lessons Poems   *Elece McKnight*

026-Where I Receive Love

The most hidden place to find
It opens the realm of love
The internal unconditional love
I'm received and embarrassed in the tender hands of love
It wasn't the kind that mankind can give
But what the creator can give
It puts one as the most loving being
Where we see the ideal
The original limitless and unconditional

Sometime it's a sorry sight
To watch and experience the violation that occurs
When someone forcefully breaking
And get it but not receiving it
Scars of hurt are sown
The kind that will never disappear
Violation of the place of love
Don't violate

Thus the only place where the love starts
Develop and grows
That sacred place
Be loved and love now and forever

I'm to love and be loved forever
I realize I'm important and,

Life Lessons Poems   *Elece McKnight*

Deserve to love and to be loved

Forever is the goal
I chant it in my heart

Forever, forever, forever
Beginning it sounded funny and silly
But I believe in loving and am loved forever
Thus the way of a chosen one

*****

027-When I Went Somewhere

It wasn't until I went somewhere
The belief and understanding I hold
And solely holding on to it
The friends I thought I had
The love I thought I was getting
When I went somewhere was different

It wasn't just somewhere
But where the love flows
Where God dwells
Where angels are everywhere
Where there was true freedom
Where the body of Christ abides
Thus when I realized

All I hold was fake
The families, friends, and love
We're not the same
As I realized it somewhere

*****

028-As I Was Graduating

Exams were over
Fear of whether I would pass or not was gone
Everything at the school was slow and boring
We had to be there
Waiting for the school year to end

The final two weeks were a period
Mixed with joy and fear
Most of the time was dedicated to getting
Everyone's address and telephone number
A focus of updating the planner was a big deal
I felt a need to set some goal for the new life

Sometimes I would feel sick to my stomach
Imagining the responsibility awaiting me
But the excitement of achievement
And looking forward to my independence
Soon took over

I remember gathering together with friends
And saying "we will be in the world, as if we were
living in space"
But I can just imagine those caring
And concerned teachers worrying about us and
Our future

So the day came

Friends were hugging and crying

Others were busy pondering their future
And the rest didn't care at all

There I was in the world
There was no connection to my dream and goals
That I had spent so much time imagining
Now I was in a real world

*****

029-Aren't You Ashamed

You use the word just like your first name
Word that was used to mock and intimidate all our ancestors
Without a choice they accept it
Not because they wanted to be called that way
Only because they were scared of their life
Aren't you ashamed?
Angry that someone said you are
How about when you call yourself
That should be used for educational purposes only
Just so you can know the history

How do you feel?
Calling yourself brother, sister, friend, uncle, aunt, niece and nephew
Sometimes even your father and mother!
You see, I'm taking long to say the word
I truly
Don't want to say it
But as I said for educational purposes
You can call them niggers?!
Do you really know what that means?
Or how it started
You could be ashamed just as I'm
Black people study and understand your history
Aren't you ashamed?
*****

030-Trip to the Kingdom Of Hell

Nasty, stinging, and smelly
Filled with horrible sounds
Sounds not of this world
Suddenly forceful beings grabbed
And dragged into the dark
Each one asking for a favor
Some mocking and laughing; horrifying laughter

I thought this was bad, yet it was only the beginning.
It was long and weary
Hunger and thirst took control
Streets were narrow, rocky, and barren.
It looked like it hadn't rained for ages
People looked shabby and were suffering
Desperation was showing through the skin
Again this was nothing compared to that destination
Home of fights, gossip, fornication, hatred and pride
There the kings and queens of this realm crowned themselves
As sons and daughters of Satan

*****

Life Lessons Poems   *Elece McKnight*

Life Lessons Poems *Elece McKnight*

Part III

Reflections on Life's Journey

From the author:

> ***Every step in life leads to a great journey.***
> ***All the journeys that we have partaken***
> ***guide us to some reflections***

001- This Is Not My Home

The place filled with anger
Hatred, jealousy, envy, lust
Thus not my home
No freedom of heart
Body bound in the bondage of sin
External and materialistic it is
I can't understand that place
Meant to believe it's my home

The place without love
Dry like barren land
And I know for sure,
This is not my home.

This is my home
My home is where I experience the essence of love
Where longing is having
Where reality of everything is experienced
Where there is true life and love
Where man and woman are
Brothers, sisters
Where plants and animals are filled
With life
Thus a place I call home.

*****

002-Somewhere I Call Home

Quiet and peaceful it is,
Such a sacred place I cherished

Made for me and only for me
Robbers and thieves can't succeed
They can steal all around me
But my home, thus for me

Walls are built within
Protected by the unknown

It has become a workshop for me
Feelings of hatred, uncertain, jealousy, betrayal
And envy have been mended

I go there whenever I feel like it
It is a bank to withdraw treasures
There, I can be at peace
Away from this world

*****

003- Truth

Truth is like the four seasons of the year,
Depending on place, environment and cultural structure
Truth in one country is not in another
Same as we expect the weather

Truth is not easily accepted by everyone
It could be the best for someone and the worst for another
Truth and its followers are flattery
They walk a lonely path
This applies to everyone, since everyone has the truth
Everyone walks a lonely path
Truth within, is the conscience we pursue
And with that!, you have the real truth.

*****

004-Its Only Here on Earth

Thus middle class
Low and high class

The poor and the rich
Thus for only here on earth

Educated or uneducated
Boundaries on every level
Black here
Whites here
Yellow here
Pretty and ugly
Just for this earth

Your country
My country
Just wasting time
Our last home, same

*****

005- Not Up To Me

Conceived, not conceived,
Boy or girl
Black, white, yellow,
Tall and short,
Beautiful/handsome or ugly
Nothing is up to me

Dead or alive,
Rain and sunny
Fertile or famine;
It sure is not up to me

Knowing the instability within me!
Changing every second, deciding the last minute,
Thank God thus not up to me

I wouldn't even want to imagine this world
If it was up to me
Chaotic and confusing
Stripping the world
Doing everything my way?
If it was up to me

Why worry! Thus not up to me

*****

006-Not Because

The life and love
Opportunities flourishing around
Not because
I was smart
Wanted to be
Desire it to

Who am I?
Not because
Thus what I wanted to be
Because of your fatherly love
Your love, mercy, and grace
Not because of me

*****

007-Agony of the Unknown

Trapped in darkness for so long
Trilling the shadows of sorrow
Looking up and down in mercy
For deliverance is far

Weary to the bone I am
How long can I still continue
As it has proven an endless struggle
That far of deliverance hoped

Countless years of hopelessness
Stunned blood of misery stream through my veins
Boosting the unwanted energy
Far beyond imagination, I waited for that deliverance

Shamelessly I screamed and yelled out loud
Making enough noise for the in-attentive
With pity they stretched out their helping hand
In the soft bosom of a soft, tender, loving hand
I couldn't hold but weep like a baby

*****

008-Why Is It So Difficult To Understand?

Basic component same
Head, neck, shoulder, legs, eyes, nose, mouth,
Ears, five senses even the blood.

In all seven continents of the world,
These basics are all the same
Babies are carried and delivered the same way
Even conceived the same
So, why is it so difficult?

*****

009-I Starved You

I always consume a lot anyway
Three times daily
Not forgetting snacks in between
Of course I got wider and wider

But yet starving you
As I got three meals,
You got nothing
As I grew fat,
You grew thinner

Little did I know
You long for three or more meals too.
You needed to grow too.

Years have flown by, just now, before I went 6 feet in the ground,
I realized
I truly starved you all those years
I saw skinny, and not mature at all

*****

010-Aren't You My Brother/Sister?

Whole-heartedly I believed you are a brother and a sister
When I look at you
I see a brother and sister
You know what?
You have a head, abdomen, legs, toes and fingers
And a face with eyes, a nose, a mouth and ears
And thus what I have too

When you are mistreated and you cry those clear tears,
I feel the same and you know what?
I have the same tears too

A mom and dad conceived you,
Carried in the womb for nine months, delivered the normal way
And you know what I was too
I can go on and on, but you know what?
I really believe you are my brother/ sister

*****

011-Supposing To Be

The way of life,
The love we get,
Thus the love we give
As we receive
We in return give back.

Just as the body functions
It takes in food
Takes out the waste
Breathes oxygen and breathes out carbon dioxide
Heart pumps blood in and out
Thus supposed to be

Thus the way to keep yourself clean
Both physically and spiritually
Just taking it in can be poisonous and dangerous
When I have enough, I'm supposed to share
It's supposed to be.

*****

012-Essence of Life

I surely believe it will come when I reach eighteen
No, it didn't happen
Then I said at age twenty-one,
No, nothing
Then after college
Well, things got worse. I then thought, well, what if I get married?
Oh yes! Everything will start unfolding
What I found out was that things started unfolding in the opposite direction
It was like a roller coaster
From bad, to worse to, more worse to the worst

With desperation, days months and years
Seem to slow down
One day I got it
It's not in age, education, money, and fame but in
Happiness and joy

*****

013-The Original Mind

Deep inside it whispers
Words not from this earth
Loving, tenderness, gentle, compassionate
And sincerity
In times of need, it offers the essentials
Not always what is pleasant and comfortable
But what is necessary to me

Though it suffers to break through the complications,
Of all the unwanted thoughts and desires
Yet strives the best of truth
Following its desire is the utmost joy to behold
All what the inner soul wishes to have
Cherishing it for eternity
A world interacting in this realm thus ideal
Filled with love, and happiness
Could be none other than the "original mind"

*****

014-The First Great Authors

Today it is a big deal
To be a great author
We get prizes and recognition

Weren't there the first great authors?
Each at list one or two even more books
With everything from short stories, to poetry, to autobiographies
Have been known but never as great authors

How then could those books compiled?
And how could all of those stories be revealed?
Sixty-six books in all?!!
What an owner they deserve.

*****

015-Freedom of My Mind

As I sit and reflect,
In an area without boundaries
A state of peace, freedom and creativity
A place to experience freedom to be
A place where thinking in seconds
Revealing the freedom within
Thus within my mind

As I visit families and friends
Penetrating the deep oceans
With all its wonders
Leaving the lonely and sorrowful

Realizing one's true self
In the freedom of the mind
The true and only freedom to be

*****

016-Priority

All my years I focused
I paid attention to that
Which I believed solely was priority

I wrote down goals as they say
First: finish high school,
Second: college,
Third: get a job,
Fourth: have a good life and a beautiful home,
Fifth: travel around the world

Somehow I got stuck on number four
That was it.
I saw absoluteness
I thought that was it
I even believed I was happy

Despite all of that
The other part of me was starving
The real me didn't touch the priority
Faraway from loving, forgiving, kindness, sacrifice,
And even knowing how to be loved

*****

017-Body Specialist

Can't be other than you
You assembled
Every part
Knowing the functions of each part of them
No one knows how long it took you
But the job was perfectly done
Everything in harmony with work
Accomplished the purpose

When sickness invades us
Dismantling the perfect order
Causing disunity within
Then we call the specialist

Who can that be?
Someone who studies the body?
Or the one who assembled it?
The one who knows every piece by its name
And exactly where it is located and its function and
the mortality rate
He is even closer
Than a phone call
You can be there much quicker
The job can be done quicker
You transcend time and space

Enabling you to answer multiple calls spontaneously
From all parts of the bible
God

No other body specialist better than you.

*****

018- Waiting for Jesus

Have been long enough
Waiting for Christ
Many have come and gone
Prophets have done their job
Still waiting for him

2000 years ago he was born
Just like an ordinary man
But not really
Many thought Joseph
And Mary's son, yet the savior
Came to his own people
But they recognized him not
Calling him names
What they didn't do, wasn't existing

Son of man had no credentials
But only the spirit of God
No paper work to show
Finally driven to the cross
Have been long enough
Waiting for him

*****

019- In Place Of

It's all in a platter
TV, calculator, computer, etc.
God given creative, desire and ambition
All wiped away

I acted like one of those invented robots
Without those man-made machines,
I'm an alien, in the world supposedly made for me

Thank goodness to the creator
The will to exist still for me

No feeling of sympathy, regrets, shame
Repentance or being sure
From love comes life
From death comes nothing
Emphasis on the machines is like,
Emphasis on dead plants
And the opposite for love

*****

020- When I Opened My Eyes

I couldn't help but cry
Tears of fear and worry
I felt sort of like walking on fire
I saw everything
Wars, hatred, resentment, jealousy, etc

I looked down, up, and sideways
I was walking, eating, working, and laughing around danger
I wanted to escape, but nowhere to go
Everywhere was something

I saw bodies deteriorating
Smell of death so close
Still I'm living, seeing but not seeing
I felt sorry for my ignorance

I begged the creator to close my eyes
I couldn't stand the sight
A deep shadow of sorrow covered my heart
I realized then why they were closed

*****

021- Forever Reunion

Though many see it as sad, unfortunate, and unbearable
And yet millions are rejoicing
To see their kin joining them
Knowing thus forever
A time they waited for so long

Departing was hard, leaving so many mourning
And yet others were looking forward to seeing them
I then realized
This is the way
The alpha and omega
The way it has been since
There forever reunion takes place

*****

022- Once Upon a Time

A world was created,
Filled with love and beauty
Creation and all things were made
And last were men and women
Reflecting the creator

Once again men and women were just people
No concept of race, creed and color
They were brothers and sisters
And the world was good

Once upon as time goes on
An act of violation was created
Defiling the love, beauty goodness and happiness
And once again man began to see black, white and yellow
Boundaries were created
And once again the good world was reflecting sin and evil
And thus the world we live in.

*****

023-A Trip to the Kingdom Of Heaven

Sweet roses like scent from the distance
Approaching were angelic sounds of music
Bright light shown revealing the angels
Whispered into my ear, *it's time to go*
I smiled and closed my eyes
Hand in hand we started
All the way I felt like I had tour guides
Showing and explaining all the different places

Trees, grass, and flowers all blooming and blossoming
All seem to be welcoming me
Birds and the wind all in harmonized tunes

Destination was white as snow
All my ancestors and friends welcomed me
Big reunion I felt
It was a place to live

*****

024-Getting High with the Most High

Immersed and intoxicated with Him
Sharing the timeless tales
In the wonders of glory and beauty
I traveled the endless golden and sparkling streets of love

To Him leaned my soul
To be lifted to the most high
The foremost highest joy
Then I started getting higher and higher
Not any kind of high
But the almighty high

It gave me the knowledge, wisdom, and beauty
Not any knowledge, wisdom, and beauty
But the one that was meant to be

Travel with me to become the highest
The highest you were meant to be
To reflect the highest of them all
Other than this, high is low
Don't do it. Its low not high

*****

025-The River

Sacred place of the ancestors
Spirits abound
Those ancient forefathers
As the pharaohs of the ancient times
Miracles and pledges were performed
Water where purity comes
Cleansing source of the past
From all the impurities

*****

026-Thank You God

Day after day it was the same
I knelt in silence
Ready for my usual selfish prayer
I then started
Help me God
Could I have…?
Please?
I then realize I'm always missing a word
Words of gratitude and love
THANK YOU GOD

*****

027-In His Bowl

We all feast in His bowl
Hungry, race, creed, white, black, rich, or poor

No discrimination
Pride,
Prejudice,
And hatred

Only love and beauty exist
We all enjoy
In our father's bowl

*****

028-I Thought This Is It

Knowing what was happening,
I lay silently, sort of, in peace
I was just waiting for the day and hour

Friends and Families all flocked
To what they thought was the last chance
It looked pretty nice
It sort of looked like a reunion

Finally I was gone
Hey! What a surprise
Vast, new, and confusing world
I started a new life
It wasn't heaven as people say
I was worried and wished I hadn't come

*****

029-God Given Credentials

Before I turned to my original credentials
As I suffer day and night
Hoping to acquire all the credentials
So I can start my job
As well as to be successful
To expose my talent

First, was to get a degree
X number of year's job experience
Type of salary
Thus before I turned to the original credential

It was a spark of the moment
When I accredited myself
I realized I could
Think, talk, walk, and touch
And all the reasoning in place
The best credentials instead
I gained my hope and confidence
As I accredited myself

*****

030-A World of Thought

While it was quiet and silent
It wasn't really quiet and silent
Another world was revealing itself
Going through today, yesterday and tomorrow

Leaving every stone turned
Moments of all aspects of life were touched
A world where just an individual can go
In that realm, no disturbances, interruptions, or competition
Usually great or poor decisions are made
A great place for great decisions
Real joy and sorrow is experienced
No judgment is passed
Thus where one can really know themselves
Though externally they are someone'
In that world, they are who they are

*****

031-Is He There

I looked up, down and sideways
I walked the miserable path
Cried nonstop
Prayed every prayer
I even learned to be patient
Enough for answers to come
I also kept a little faith and hope
But I can't help but ask
Is he there?

Asking this but also filled with fear
What if he says no?
But instead
I'm here
Look around
Air, trees, humans, animals, and the rest of the creation
If no, the rest is no
Am I there?

*****

032-What a Miserable God I am

Woo woo!! what?!
What a what?
What I miserable God I am

I created Them in My Own image. Gen1:26:27
Blessed Then with equality in their uniqueness
Uniqueness to fulfill their responsibilities
Watching them growing was a joy
Anticipating the joy to continue

Before long, the joyful God was a miserable One

Fights, hatred, Bigotry, Jealous wars entered the land
Beauty was turned ugly
Very little signs of a better world

All I can do is cry with pain
Misery filled my heart
From then until a better world

*****

033-When I Turned Off All Lights

It was a whole new world
A world of imagining and reflecting
It was the other lights being turned on
Lights of beauty and love

All the five senses were kindled
Bit by bit they started showing their brilliance
I recall taking my time to perceive
What was in front of me?
I had to feel every object then
Determined to find out what it was
Learning to taste without seeing
Recognizing people through voices
Smelling foods of every kind
And even sensing danger before it was on me
My brains worked thousands of times faster

I then realized the reality
Of both worlds; physically and spiritually
All of the spiritual lights were off and twice the physical
I realized what I have been missing
When I turned off all of the lights

*****

034-I'm Blind

Every day with the same routine I wake up
Wash, dress, maybe a prayer and start breakfast
I couldn't imagine how blind I was

That morning I could be in an accident
Could be sick in the hospital
Maybe ready to die
But I was so blind that I couldn't see

A beloved one just dies
Too blind I wasn't prepared
To know what was coming

I see but not see
My brothers' and sisters' feelings so hurt
I couldn't even see that

*****

035-Why Black And White

First was God
Then the world and the creation

Right in the midst was two beings
Known as Adam and Eve

Only God knows how these beings looked
Angelic words were in existence
Known for its goodness

In his willingness the world grew
Cultures, Races and Languages were formed

Then once upon a time two beings were reformed and transformed
And made a new

Now there are white, blacks, and yellows

With all the love and creativity He gave us,
We started to draw images
Angels……………White
Satan, Witches and anything representing
Evil……………..Black

And so it came to pass

Life Lessons Poems *Elece McKnight*

Anything white represents cleanliness, pureness, and goodness
Anything evil, satanic, devilish, and totally unwanted was black
Why disturb the order of creation
The once called beautiful sons and daughters are now enemies

Why black, white, yellow or anything else?

*****

036-Old Self

Now I come before you
Loaded with everything except
Something I didn't know about
That basket full of
Hatred
Pain
Ignorance
Selfishness
Pride
Disrespect
Now I come before you
Turning 180 degrees
Now I come before you
Tired and weary
Now I come before you
Receive all of me, lord
Lead me through the light

No more crying
No more worry
No more regrets
Only love and glory
Dignity, respect, ownership can abide
Finally I come

*****

037-Rather Take a Path

There were roads, streets and highways
They all look better, faster, and even safer
But I'd rather use a path

It was thorny rocky and sandy
It was scary and dark
It was in the midst of the woods
I could hardly see
Despite it all, I'd rather use the path

Tempting voices came to me and said
Look at her
She is still using the path
In this day and time
They laughed and mocked me
Still I'd rather use the path

Ahead of me was a light
A light of hope
Then I knew the path was the right way to take
I then determined to use the path

*****

038-A Knock at My Door

Knock! Knock! Knock!!!
I heard a knock
It was the familiar knock I knew
I did not want to open the door
I was sick and tired of the evil doers
Of the world

It pounded so hard that finally I opened the door
It was a familiar face
It was the face of the most high
Wounded and bloody

I tried to clean it but it was hard
Blood kept oozing like a spring of water
I couldn't comfort the pain
And agony coming from the most high

A whispering voice came from afar
Why are you trying to destroy me?
So frightened and confused I asked
Who are you?

Then I heard, "your father, mother, brother, sister,
uncle, aunt, cousin, nephew, niece
I fell on the ground in tears

Life Lessons Poems   *Elece McKnight*

I wept so hard then I remembered

When Paul was going to Damascus

It was the voice that talked to me
It is this voice talking today

*Inspired by the speech **"why there should be war"***
January 28 2003

*****

039- This Little Light of Mine

Imagine the deep dark room!
Just bring one candle,
It feels like the electric bulb was turned on
This little light of mine,
Thus the small things each one of us has

The Love
The Smile
The Laughter
The Kiss
The Care
The Sympathy
The Understanding and,
The Cooperation etc

These little lights,
That brightens the whole world
Seek your little light

LET IT SHINE!
LET IT SHINE!
LET IT SHINE!

*****

040-Gathered For the Word

In unison we await
Eagerly and attendant
A day that most people remember
For what reason, I don't know
Though we all gather for the word

It was the word of life
To give life and realization
As bodies gathered
Minds were scattered
Praising and worshipping
All by the flesh
Still gathered for the word

Word that should lead us to heaven
Word that should redirect us
Word that was in the beginning
We were still gathered for the word
Johnny was looking at woman,
Bob worried about his finances
And so on and so on
We were still gathered for the word

Now the church was full
Spirit seemed to be high

Yet each one taking a different path
Some straight to hell
Others somewhere mediocre

One or none to heaven
All this in church
Still gathering for the word

I don't know if it was the same word
That same word of life
Well I'm confused
I'm still gathered for the word

*****

041-Slave to a Belief

Could be in anything
Religion, racism, theory, etc...
Beginning it's alright
It builds confident self-esteem and sense of being

Slavery comes like a thief
Crouching behind a belief
Soon you are stuck and unable to do without
Decision and accomplishments starts to be based on a belief

It comes like this,
My religion doesn't say that
We are better than that race
We believe we can do better

Oh! Please free yourself from that belief
I learned a different theory
The bible says,
That Sabbath was made for man but not man for the Sabbath.
We are not meant to be slaves to a belief

*****

042-The Source

Whether we know it or not
It doesn't matter
Rivers flow
Meandering place to place
And country to country
With all the responsibilities it has,
Water to wash, drink, and feed the plants
Even that, we agree there is a source
Or even try to find it
Either way, we know, there is a source
Same as electricity
We turn it on, and see
And believe we have electricity
Where is the source?
Though unseen,
Undoubtedly
The source is there.
The creator

*****

043-The Original Mind

Deep inside it whispers
Words not from this earth
Loving, tenderness, gentle, compassionate
And sincerity
In times of need, it offers the essentials
Not always what is pleasant and comfortable
But what is necessary to me

Though it suffers to break through the complications,
Of all the unwanted thoughts and desires
Yet strives the best of truth
Following its desire is the utmost joy to behold
All what the inner soul wishes to have
Cherishing it for eternity
A world interacting in this realm thus ideal
Filled with love, and happiness
Could be none other than the "original mind"

*****

Life Lessons Poems   *Elece McKnight*

Life Lessons Poems   *Elece McKnight*

Website: www.TheVisionProduction.com
Email: thevisionproduction@hotmail.com

Facebook: http://facebook/TheVisionProduction2014
Twitter: http://twitter/TheVisionProduc
Dribbble : http://dribbble.com/TheVisionProduction
Linkedin: http://lnkd.in/gQ-StG

Life Lessons Poems   *Elece McKnight*

www.ingramcontent.com/pod-product-compliance
Lightning Source LLC
Chambersburg PA
CBHW060834050426
42453CB00008B/692